Scroll Saw
Basics

M000105435

Scroll Saw
Basics

Marc Berner

4880 Lower Valley Road · Atglen, PA · 19310

Other Schiffer books on related subjects
54 3-D Scroll Saw Patterns. Frank Pozsgai. ISBN: 0764300369. $12.95
125 Christmas Ornament Patterns for the Scroll Saw. Arthur L. Grover.
   ISBN: 0764303236. $14.95.

Schiffer Books are available at special discounts for bulk purchases for sales promo-
tions or premiums. Special editions, including personalized covers, corporate imprints,
and excerpts can be created in large quantities for special needs. For more information
contact the publisher:

Published by Schiffer Publishing Ltd.
4880 Lower Valley Road
Atglen, PA 19310
Phone: (610) 593-1777; Fax: (610) 593-2002
E-mail: Info@schifferbooks.com

For the largest selection of fine reference books on this and related subjects,
please visit our web site at **www.schifferbooks.com**
We are always looking for people to write books on new and related subjects. If
you have an idea for a book please contact us at the above address.

This book may be purchased from the publisher.
Include $5.00 for shipping.
Please try your bookstore first.
You may write for a free catalog.

In Europe, Schiffer books are distributed by
Bushwood Books
6 Marksbury Ave.
Kew Gardens
Surrey TW9 4JF England
Phone: 44 (0) 20 8392 8585; Fax: 44 (0) 20 8392 9876
E-mail: info@bushwoodbooks.co.uk
Website: www.bushwoodbooks.co.uk

Acknowledgments

I would like to acknowledge the Marc Adams School of Woodworking.

Copyright © 2009 by Marc Berner and Schiffer Publishing
Library of Congress Control Number: 2009932313

All rights reserved. No part of this work may be reproduced or used in any form or
by any means—graphic, electronic, or mechanical, including photocopying or information
storage and retrieval systems—without written permission from the publisher.
   The scanning, uploading and distribution of this book or any part thereof via the Internet
or via any other means without the permission of the publisher is illegal and punishable by
law. Please purchase only authorized editions and do not participate in or encourage the
electronic piracy of copyrighted materials.
   "Schiffer," "Schiffer Publishing Ltd. & Design," and the "Design of pen and ink well" are
registered trademarks of Schiffer Publishing Ltd.

Designed by RoS
Type set in Cambria/Zurich BT

ISBN: 978-0-7643-3377-4
Printed in China

Contents

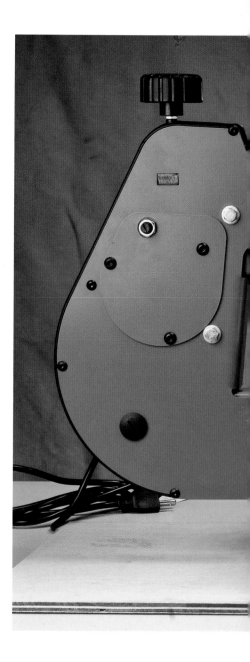

Why Buy a Scroll Saw?

For a long time, the versatility of the scroll saw was one of the best-kept secrets in the woodworking field. Most woodworkers own or have used one for a project in their shops. Today, the word is getting out and now the scroll saw is one of the most popular, best selling tools on the market.

When using a scroll saw, you can successfully complete projects using techniques and cuts that no other tool can manage. Using the proper blade, you can cut the most intricate pattern. This saves time and money on every project.

With a scroll saw, you can cut into a piece of wood, travel 180 degrees around the block, and come back out again at the original cut made by the blade. People use their saws to create widely varied projects, ranging from multi-pieced model planes to wood art created in a single cut.

Whether you wish to use soft balsa wood or the hardest of woods known to humanity, the scroll saw can cut it all. You can cut plastics as intricately as wood with a smooth finish. Saws can even cut non-ferrous metal up to 3/8th of an inch thick.

Most importantly, a scroll saw can do one thing that no other saw can manage: the scroll saw can make inside cuts. Simply drill a hole into the material you want to cut, just a little larger than the actual blade you are using, unhook the blade from the upper blade holder, run it through the hole and reconnect, and you are ready to cut. No other power tool has this feature

Cutting with a Scroll Saw is Different

It is important to note that using a scroll saw requires more knowledge and practice than do the other saws you may have encountered. With every other saw you put the wood against a fence or some type of jig and simply push it into the rigid blade. However, to use the a scroll saw properly, you actually turn the wood around the blade, following the outline of the pattern without the guidance of any fence or support.

Scroll Saw Styles & History

One identifies scroll saws by both measuring the distance between the blade and the back supports and by its construction. Because you can only turn around material that is under a certain size before it hits the back of the saw, the size is determined by measuring this critical distance. The most common sizes are 14 inch, 16 inch, 20 inch, 21 inch, 24 inch, 26 inch, and 31 inch. The four types of saw construction are parallel arm, C-arm style, rigid arm, and double parallel link.

Scroll saws originated in the sixteenth century, when they consisted of two wooden boards connected at one end where the blade was. At the other end the boards were connected with two threaded rods so they could be tightened to keep a constant pressure on the blade at all times. At that time they were called "walking beams saws." Moving forward several centuries, in the early 1930s, Delta came out with the rigid arm saw. This made it easier to keep the blade going straight up and down. The Delta scroll saw had an arm length of above 24 inches. In the late 1930s, the C arm variation was designed. This very popular C arm saw continued to be made into the 1990s. Almost every manufacturer has now turned around and started making saws very close to the original design of the 1500s with the parallel arms. Now the two saws being made are a "Constant Tension Parallel Arm saw" and "Double Parallel Link."

Saw Anatomy

All saws have one feature in common: a protractors under the table so you can tell how far to tilt your table. But after that, they all vary in each feature in one small way to another. One saw, the Excalibur, has a table that is stationary but the head tilts.

The blade holder is the one feature on the scroll saw that has the greatest variation from model to model. Blade holders range from models that are so sophisticated that they require a special key – a key that you cannot buy from any other manufacture – to hold or release the blade to holders that simply require the push from a finger to open and shut them on the blade.

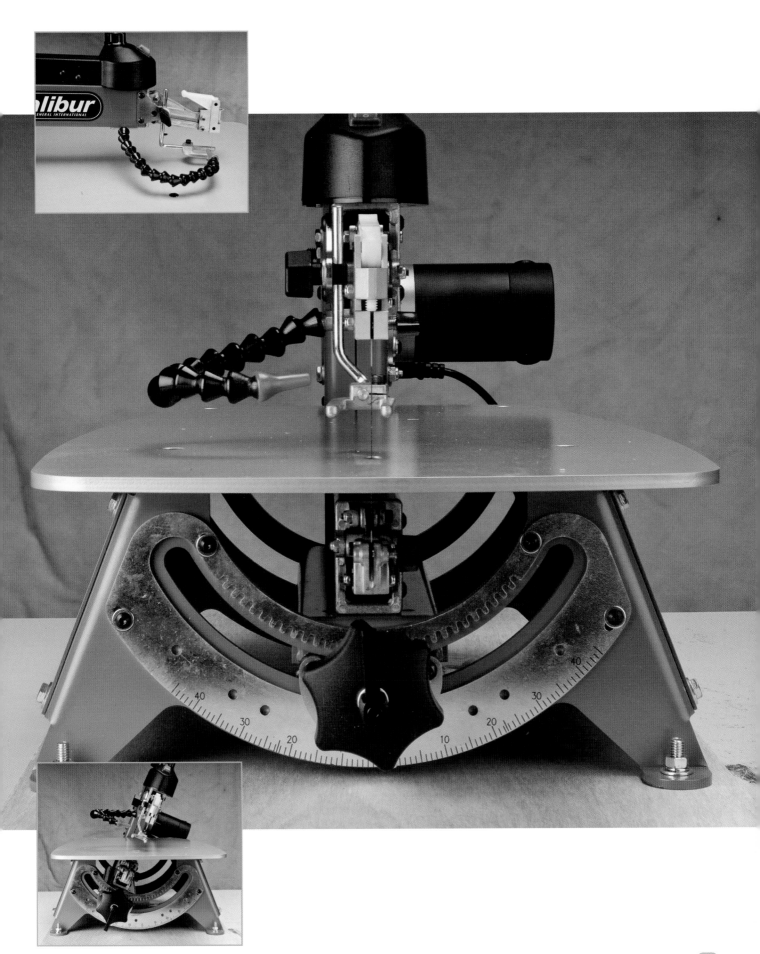

Tension Devices

The tension devices on each saw are very similar. They are either on the back or the front of every saw. Looking at the two most common styles, the parallel arm styles of Delta, Dewalt, Dremel, Excalibur, Hegner, R.B.I. Hawk, Ryobi, Sakura, Sears, Shop Smith and Total Shop have the tension rods at the back or front of the saw. The tension screw on a C frame style is up front.

The tensions on the rigid arm are similar to the C frame style by being up front, but work under a totally different concept. After the blade is pulled down by a cam under the bottom blade holder, the blade is supposed to be pulled up by a spring in the upper blade holder. The main problem with this style is the blade tension doesn't really meet the need for all cutting applications. In operation, the cam actually starts pushing the blade up before the blade spring can pull up and keep the blade tension tight. This usually causes excessive blade breakage.

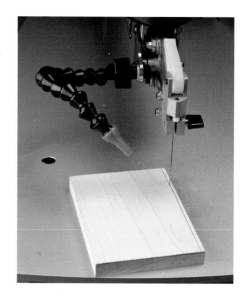

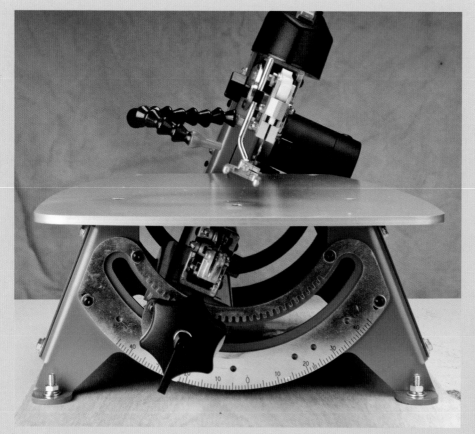

Table Protractors

Every saw comes with a protractor on the lower part of the table. These protractors always have to be adjusted when you first use your saw. Usually there is a screw you can turn to make sure the marker is pointing to zero when the table is at a 90° angle to the blade.

First check the table and make sure it is at 90° to the blade. You can do this by taking a thick piece of wood and make a short cut into it. Then turn the wood over and place it behind the blade. Make sure you turn the wood over so the top becomes the bottom and the bottom becomes the top. With the wood behind the blade, you can see if the blade matches up with the cut. If not, you loosen the table and adjusted it back half the distance between the blade cut and the blade against the wood. If you go any farther back than half, the blade will be angled the other way. Make a second cut now and check it again. When you turn the wood over following the cut, it should line up exactly with the blade. Now set the protractor.

Some saws can only tilt to the left because the motor is on the right. Others tilt both ways. All saws tilt 45° to the left. Those that tilt to the right, tilt between 15° and 45° to the right.

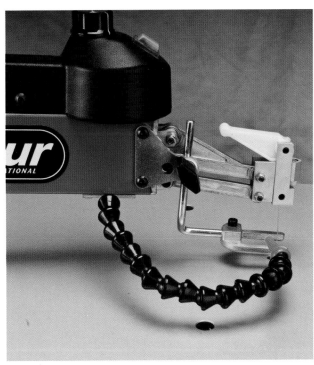

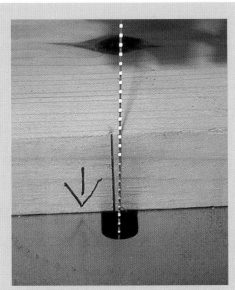

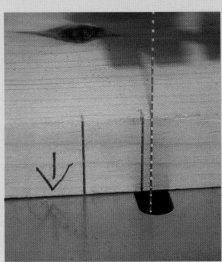

Motors

All of the saws that come with a motor are equipped with totally enclosed fan-cooled motors. With the very fine dust that is produced during cutting, the enclosed motors last longer. These motors vary in size. They may also be either AC or AC/DC motors. An AC/DC motor is used primarily when you have a variable speed motor, but not all manufacturers use one. The motors range in size from 1.9 volt to 2.4 volt.

Features of Saws

Most of the saws today look alike. So, what are the features that set them apart? The speed at which the saws run is one distinguishing feature. The length of the blade stroke is another. Some saws come with a lamp. They may come with or without dust blowers. Table size varies and the table shape ranges from oval to banjo style. Some saws are tabletop models without legs and others are designed to stand on the floor. Beginner models take pin-end and plain-end blades. The more expensive models take only plain-end blades. Pin end blades are thicker and have a hole cut with a pin pushed through to attache the blade into the saw. Plain end blades have no pins in them and, due to this, they are much thinner. The smallest pin end blade is thicker than the largest plain end blade. See the blade chart on pages 18 and 19 for details.

Saw Speeds

Most scroll saws have a single speed of approximately 1750 strokes per minute. This may vary by size and manufacture, due to the size and power of the motor. It is not uncommon for saws to come with at least two speeds. The top-of-the-line saws come with variable speeds.

Speed controls vary from saw to saw. Some saws come with an electronically controlled, rheostat-like device. On others the speed is changed by changing a belt or pulley. And some just have a two-speed switch.

Experiment with how different speeds aid in the ease of cutting. You will have more control in cutting intricate patterns at lower speeds.

If you are trying to learn how to cut with a scroll saw, put your saw on low speed if it is a two speed or on a medium speed if it has a variable speed control. Why start at a low or medium speed? Remember when you first learned how to drive your car? You didn't start right up and roar off at 55 mph the first time you sit behind the wheel. Just a little turn of the wheel at 55 mph and the first timer will be off the road. Well, the same goes for cutting with a scroll. When you aren't sure if you can stay on the line, perhaps because of your inexperience with the saw or due to the intricacy of the pattern, just slow the saw down. With the motor moving at a slower speed, the blade won't cut as fast and you can follow the pattern more easily. This is especially important when you are first learning to cut. Use the slower or middle speed and you will have greater success staying on the line. When I have to cut something with difficult turns or small pieces, I will slow my saw down for greater control. The one bad thing about running the saw on slow is the blade tends to grab if you push too fast.

Saw Stroke

The stroke or movement of the blade up and down varies from 5/8th of an inch to 1 full inch. If your saw has a short stroke, it will not use as much of the blade when cutting. This will have the tendency to burn wood quicker and wear out the blade much faster. This tendency to burn and wear shows up especially when cutting plastic. It will melt together faster on a short stroke. The short stroke is usually used to help stop vibration. If the stroke is longer, you use more blade; this long stroke helps stop burning and will cut plastic more cleanly.

Dust Blower

When I bought my *first* scroll saw it did not have a dust blower, which is probably the single most valuable feature you need. It keeps the dust off of the pattern line and out of the way when you are trying to cut. Without a dust blower, you will not be able to cut for long before you realize that a blower is a must.

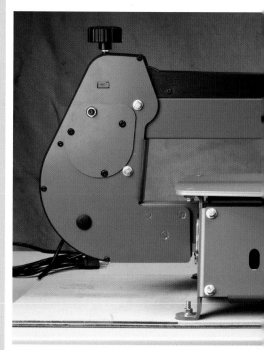

Table Size

Each manufacturer has an idea of what the tabletop size ought to be. It doesn't really matter if that tabletop is really large or not, because you can always make a false table that will be any size you need. (See false table.)

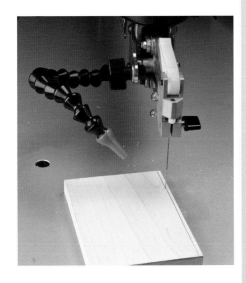

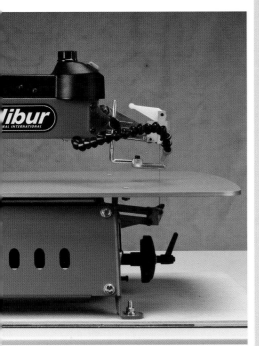

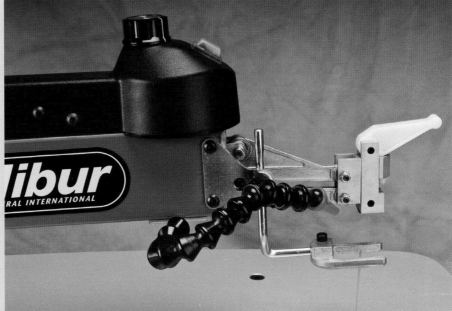

Blade Holders

This is the single feature that most sets saws apart. You will not want to use a saw that only takes pin-end blades. You will want one that takes straight, plain-end blades. The ability to easily change the plain-end blades makes all the difference.

You will also want what is called a "quick release" on the top blade holder of your saw. Although it is not necessary to have a quick release on the bottom of the blade, it is nice to have at least a thumb nut for easy removal. If you have a saw that uses an Allen wrench or a key of some kind, replace them with thumb nut or wing nut styles for easy blade removal.

The quick release is essential for both inside cuts and for cutting fretwork and project time can be cut in half with its use.

All quick releases work under the same principal, with a small tension release and a blade release mechanism. But each manufacturer has its idea of how this works. The quick release for the blade and tension release is all encompassed into one simple step on the Dewalt. Their system has eliminated one step completely. The tension knob up front also acts as the quick release. Release this and then you just have the thumb nut to release the blade. All other saws have the small quick release that is separate from the main tension release. You can get a quick release lever for tension on the back of your saw from RBI Industries. But you still have to release the blade up front.

Table or Floor Models

The choice is really up to the user, but most tabletop saws have a stand available. I like to be able to sit on a stool at the saw. To make the stool height comfortable for working for protracted periods at the saw, I cut the legs off to a height that allows my arms to remain at a 90° angle to the table. If you have a tabletop model, this can be hard unless you have a special table made to adjust the height.

Accessories

There are only three suggested accessories for a scroll saw.

1. Using a foot pedal with your saw is a must. Use the type where it is on when you have your foot on it and off as soon as you lift it off. Do not get the kind where you just click it on and off. You will move your foot off and hunt for it when you are trying to turn it off fast. While cutting you have both hands on the material. With a foot pedal you essentially have a third hand controlling whether your saw is running or not. This really is important, in case your hand slips while turning and the wood jumps. Then what if the blade breaks? You will probably stop the saw the second you lose control or the blade breaks because it scares you. You will find that your foot will come off the pedal the second either event occurs.

I cut large projects for lawn ornaments. The foot pedal comes in handy because I can slide the pedal out away from my saw and still control the power

a magnifying lens at the same time; there are two styles out there of light and lens combos. Both attach to the stand or the bench next to your saw. I prefer attaching it to the bench and then swing it to the saw so I don't hit the arm with the wood while cutting.

One model has a florescent bulb around the lens. This one is usually a larger model. The other is slightly smaller, but I prefer it because it uses an incandescent bulb. I will move the lens out of the way when it is not needed and continue to use the light as an additional light source while cutting. If you have not tried to cut with a magnifying glass, you will need to take some time getting familiar with it. Remember this, "Whatever your eyes can see, your hands can conceive." The lens makes the line you are trying to cut look as wide as a railroad. You will actually feel that you are having a hard time following the line at first because of the way the magnifier enlarges your mistakes. Cut with the lens, have faith, and then look

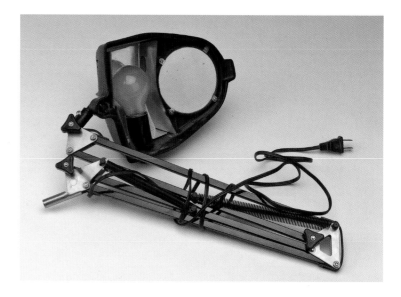

while holding the large board. I am always starting and stopping to back out and start a new cut because of the size of the wood. **Do not** use the pedals that have a rheostat in them. I have done so, and whenever I used them, they burned up the motor. If your saw does not come with a variable speed motor, don't try to make it one by purchasing that foot pedal with a rheostat.

2. Some saws come with a lamp. I have found that these usually begin to vibrate after a short time and the bulb breaks a lot. You can get a light and

at the finished project out from under the magnifier and you will discover the cuts actually look great.

3. New saws come with a quick release now. Until a couple of years ago they were an option. You should have one on your saw. The quick release mechanism will actually cut down the time it takes to change or remove the blade for inside cuts by more then half. Check with your saw supplier and get one for your older saw if it does not have one. If you cannot find an appropriate quick release for your machine, you can call Seyco Sales in Texas. They have quick-change holders for any saw made.

Maintenance and Safety

The number one rule in any shop is always wear safety glasses. This cannot be stressed enough.

One time a student brought in his saw and, when he turned it on, the sound it made indicated something had to be loose. After making an initial check of all the obvious bolts and other usual suspects, and finding nothing, I checked the blade tension. I quickly discovered the blade tension was way too loose. Saws are built to be in alignment and to have tension on the blade. We both could hear the difference in the saw when the tension was right. Proper tension on the blade has been achieved when the blade will only move back 1/8" when cutting.

Remember to install the blade with the teeth facing down. If you don't, you will be made instantly aware of your mistake when the blade hits the wood. That improperly installed blade will try to pick up the wood with each stroke.

I have seen people wear paper masks while cutting to keep sawdust out of their noses, throats, and lungs. One reason for this is that many saws with factory installed dust blowers are mounted in such a way that they are blowing the dust right into your face when you first use it. If this is the way your blower is set up, I would recommend changing it for health reasons. To send the sawdust elsewhere, and out of your face, take some copper tubing and bend it into a half moon shape. Then slip it over or into the plastic tube blowing the air and direct it off to the side. With such a simple remedy you would think the manufacture would fix this. Without the dust blowing to the side you will see a fine dust all over the front of you.

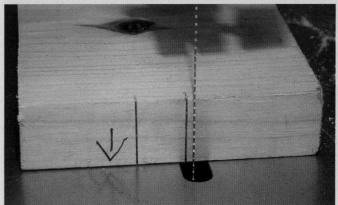

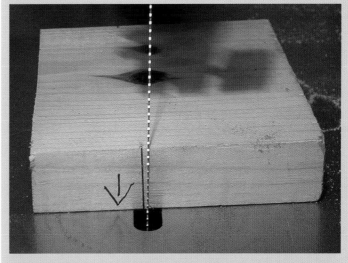

Setting Up Your Saw

When you take your saw out of the box, you will notice a rather large blade in the saw. This blade is usually one that is large for shipping. The blade is larger so it will not break during shipment. This helps keep the saw arms from coming loose from blade breakage. Throw it away. Put in a number 5 blade and practice cutting with some pine.

However, before cutting, check your table and make sure it is flat. By flat, I mean that the table is at a 90° angle to the blade for straight up and down cuts. You will probably have to adjust the protractor on the front. They are not always accurate when set at the factory. There is a small pointer adjustable by a screw. Loosen the pointer and then move it to 0 once your blade is set at 90 degrees to the table.

Some saws come with a table that is rougher than others. You can do a couple of things to make the rougher tables work better. First, you can sand the table surface smooth. Second, you can place a false table over it.

Blades

Saws do not cut the wood, **"the blade cuts the wood."** The saw is just the vehicle that moves the blade. When you cut, if you use the same blade on the same piece of wood, you will get the same finish if you cut at the same speed. If you try to push it faster through the wood in one saw and slower through another, you will get a difference.

There are two different types of blades, the Pin end and Plain end. Some lower end saws will take both types of blade. The more expensive saws take only the plain end blades. This should give you a hint. The plain end blades are the ones you want to use. They last a lot longer and give you the finish you desire. The only reason you would use pin end blades is if you can't find the plain end blade holders. And if you can find them, go out and buy several to use with plain end blades.

Because of the lack of popularity of the less durable pin end blades, there is not a great selection among them. They come in just two styles with the same style of tooth. They are skip tooth and skip tooth with reverse teeth on the bottom. (See blade chart pgs. 18-19)

The following are the different styles of plain end blades.

    Wood blades
    Skip tooth.
    Double tooth.
    Crown
    Spiral
    Reverse
    Metal blades (Blade charts)

How is a Blade Made?

First let's talk about how a blade is made. Not all blades are stamped out as many believe. As a matter of fact, only pin end blades and the "old fashioned" wide and thick blades used in old spring tension scroll saws are stamped or, more correctly, "notched." The thin and narrow plain end blades, so popular for today's parallel arm and C-arm scroll saws, have skip teeth, which are "milled" into soft steel. As the milling cutter moves across the material to form the teeth, the flow of steel removal is in one direction. As a consequence, a slight bur may be formed. When you put the blade in your scroll saw, the bur is on the right side of the blade. This is why it will not cut in a straight line without turning your work piece slightly. The bur makes it drift to the right. So keep this in mind when cutting. Always keep the material you want to save for your finished project to the left side of the blade. The right side cuts with a slightly rougher finish than the left. Remember that scroll saw blades are made for cutting radii, not just straight lines. (Refer to chart 1.)

Milled blades come in three different styles. The most common blades are called skip tooth. (Refer to chart I) The second most common blade is the double tooth. The double tooth blade has a smaller space between two teeth, then a larger space before the next two teeth. (Refer to chart 2.) Perhaps the best cutting scroll saw blades on the market have ground teeth. Because the teeth are ground twice in hardened steel with a fine grit stone, the blades are sharper, last longer, and cut in a straight line. Remember that, even with these stone ground blades, they will still cut smoother on the left then on the right. These blades are called Precision Ground Tooth, or P.G.T. blades. P.G.T. blades will cut where the regular milled blades might burn.

They also cut through wood faster because of the sharpness imparted to the blade by the stone grind process. These blades come in just three sizes. They are #5, #7, and #9. (Refer to chart.)

The newest blade available is the Crown Tooth. These blades are milled and you cannot tell which is the top or the bottom. If you look you will see each tooth cuts on the up and down stroke. You can only tell by the direction the blade drifts while cutting. What does this blade do for you? It almost totally eliminates the splintering or breaking of wood on the bottom of the cut.

Blade Tension

After proper blade selection, proper blade tension is the next most important issue. Have you been told that the blade should make a high C when you pluck it with your finger? I haven't found this to be true. Different thicknesses of blades make different tones. Besides, do you know many woodworkers, working around the noise of the scroll saw all day, who are not tone deaf? So, forget the sound of the blade when plucked. As stated above, when you have the blade properly tightened, it should not move back more then 1/8th of and inch when you push material into the blade. *Most people run the blade too loose.* This 1/8th inch rule of thumb works especially well when you are making inside cuts, as when you are producing fretwork. Besides, with the blade going through the wood you can't pluck the blade and hear a sound anyway.

If your blade breaks in the middle without having been heavily used, the blade tension was most likely too loose. If you are cutting thicker material, the blade has to be set for the proper tension or your work will not come apart. Here is an example of what I mean: Have you ever cut thick material and the wood has a hard time sliding out at the cut in either direction? This occurred because the blade was too loose and when you turned the wood, the blade actually cut in a half moon shape rather than making a uniform, straight cut through the thick wood. You want the blade to stay as straight as possible while you cut.

At other times, the blade will actually cut off in an unexpected direction when you wanted it to stay on the line. This also occurs when the blade tension is loose and you have it bent to one side or the other. The blade is either going to break under these conditions or snap back where it would cut and you are lucky it didn't break.

Remember this one thing about a quick release. Every time you take the blade out of the holder and put it back in, it will not have the same tension. You will not get the blade in the same position as it was when you took it out. You will have to check the tension and usually make it a little tighter.

Now for the spiral blades: They, like the others blades, have to be very tight. Spiral blades rasp their way through while cutting. Spiral blades are used when roughness is not an issue. There is one important characteristic of spiral blades that you need to know. When you put them in and tighten them up properly and cut about 1 to 2 inches and stop, you will notice that some of the tension is gone. Spiral blades and spiral blades alone will lose tension in the first 1 to 2 inches of cut because the heat makes them elongate. They are like springs and the will stretch the first time you use them. Once you have made the initial cut and have tightened them for the second time, you can use them again and again without further stretching. This characteristic of spiral blades is why so many people do not like them. When they are loose they seem to have a mind of their own. Keep them tight, however, and you will have much more success. This is the only blade that cuts in any direction you push the wood into it. It works great when cutting large material. You do not have to turn the wood around the blade. The only draw back to the spiral blade is that it cuts rough on all sides. However, in the cases where spiral blades are generally used, roughness is not an issue. You will not care if the side of your cut is smooth or not.

Blade Life

As previously stated, your blade will break prematurely if you run it too loose. Here is why this happens. You stretch the blade when you tighten the it from top to bottom. Then, if you do not tighten it enough, when you push the material into the blade, you bend and stretch the blade from front to back as well. This combined double bend or flex really weakens the blade, and quickly. If kept really tight, however, the blade will not stretch from front to back, or left to right.

Keeping this in mind, you quickly realize that your blade will not last as long when you do a lot of fretwork. Every time you take a blade out, then reinstall it, that repeated stretching shortens the life of the blade. Each reinstallation stretches the metal a little more. Because of this, when I am done cutting on a saw I *do not loosen the blade.* I have not found an adverse effect on any saw that I have owned in which I have left the blade tight. One saw I have had now for twelve years. Once, when talking to a manufacturer about why they suggested loosening the blades, they said, "because they do the same on band saws." However, it is not necessary to take the blade out of your scroll saw, so leave it tight.

Sometimes people break the blade right at the blade holder. This usually occurs when they have tightened the blade holder too much. It happens when using an Allen wrench or another tool. You squeeze the metal too tight and while the blade flexes during cutting the stress is at the holder.

Scroll Saw Blade Selection Chart

OLSON®
www.olsonsaw.com

Material | **Finish**

Legend: Recommended ▓ | Can Use ▒ | Not Recommended ☐

Material/Finish column headers: Hard Wood 1/2"–3/4" | Hard Wood to 1/2" | Soft Wood to 1/2"–3/4" | Soft Wood to 1 1/2" | Veneer/Thin Wood to 3/16" | Plywood | MDF | Particle Board | Corian 1/8"–1/2" | Plastic 1/2"–3/4" | Non Ferrous Metal | Aluminum | Smooth | Splinter-Free | Medium

Olson UPC No.	Univ. No.	Width	Thickness	TPI/No. Rev.	Tooth Style	Pilot Hole	Application	Corian	Plastic
PGT® Precision Ground Tooth (The Best!)									
45502	5RG	.045"	.018"	12/9	Skip	1/16"	Most accurate and durable, lasts three to four times longer than other scroll saw blades, ultra smooth finish, straight or close radius cutting, splinter-free with clean edges on top and bottom surfaces	1/8"	1/8"
45702	7RG	.047"	.018"	10/7	Skip	1/16"		3/8"	3/8"
45902	9RG	.049"	.018"	8/6	Skip	1/16"		1/2"	3/4"
49502	5RG	.045"	.018"	12/8	Double	1/16"		1/8"	1/8"
49702	7RG	.047"	.018"	105/8	Double	1/16"		3/8"	3/8"
49902	9RG	.049"	.018"	9/6	Double	1/16"		1/2"	3/4"
Crown Tooth™									
62000	2/0	.024"	.011"	20	Crown	1/32"	Veining, line art, extreme radius cutting	1/8"	1/8"
62200	2	.026"	.013"	20	Crown	3/64"	Extreme radius, delicate fretwork	1/8"	1/8"
62300	3	.032"	.014"	16	Crown	3/64"	Tight radius fretwork	1/8"	3/16"
62500	5	.038"	.016"	16	Crown	1/16"	Close radius fretwork, general purpose	1/8"	1/4"
62700	7	.045"	.017"	11	Crown	1/16"	Close radius, general purpose	1/8"	3/4"
62900	9	.053"	.018"	6	Crown	1/16"	General purpose, multi-layers	1/8"	3/4"
63200	12	.065"	.024"	6	Crown	5/64"	Heavy duty for faster cuts	1/2"	3/4"
Reverse Tooth									
44002	2/0	.022"	.010"	28/21	Skip	1/32"	Veining, line art, extreme radius cutting		
44302	2R	.029"	.012"	20/14	Skip	3/64"	Extreme radius, delicate fretwork		
44602	5R	.038"	.016"	12.5/9	Skip	3/64"	Close radius fretwork, general purpose		
44802	7R	.047"	.017"	11.5/8	Skip	1/16"	Close radius, general purpose		
45002	9R	.054"	.019"	11.5/8	Skip	1/16"	General purpose, multi-layers		
45302	12R	.062"	.024"	9.5/6	Skip	5/64"	Heavy duty for faster cuts		
42002	–	.100"	.022"	9/5	Skip	1/8"	For cutting thick wood and multi-layers		
Flat End Spiral									
46800	2	–	.035"	41	–	5/64"	Medium speed and medium finish of hard and soft wood, plaster, and wallboard		
46900	4	–	.041"	36	–	7/64"			
Spiral									
46100	0	–	.032"	46	–	3/64"	Bevel cut letters, etc., medium finish fretwork and workpieces too large to turn		
46300	2	–	.035"	41	–	5/64"			
46500	4	–	.041"	36	–	7/64"			
NEW! Mach Speed™									
64302	3R	.032"	.014"	13/7	Skip	3/64"	Accurate tight radius cuts	1/8"	1/8"
64502	5R	.038"	.016"	13/7	Skip	5/64"	Steady close radius cuts	1/8"	1/8"
64702	7R	.046"	.017"	8/6	Skip	7/64"	Fast close radius cuts	3/8"	3/8"
64902	9R	.055"	.018"	8/6	Skip	3/64"	Fast close radius cuts in thicker wood	1/2"	3/4"

Skip Tooth PGT

Double Tooth PGT

PGT® blades have razor sharp reverse teeth with widely spaced gullets for cutting straighter, faster, smoother, more accurately. PGT's minimize burning & provide the ultimate sand-free, splinterless finish with a clean edge. Double tooth style is especially good for cutting hard woods.

Hint! Reverse Tooth blades work best with 1-2 reverse teeth showing above the table on the upstroke! Adjust blade in holder or trim when necessary.

Unique **Crown Tooth** blades cut on both up and down strokes. Two way cutting action provides a smooth, splinterless finish, and clean edges. When worn, the blade can be turned over for cutting with a fresh set of teeth!

Hint! Tension blade properly! With reasonable force the center of the blade should not move more than 1/8" front to back. Too little tension weakens performance.

Reverse Tooth blades have skip style teeth and reverse teeth that eliminate underside tear-out and provide a smooth, splinter-free finish.

Hint! More teeth per inch provide a finer cut (good for soft wood). Less TPI provide a coarser cut (good for hard wood). Use the highest number blade for your application (larger blades are more durable).

Flat End Spiral blades are the same as regular spiral blades, but with flat ends for easier blade installation and retention. Offered in the two most popular sizes.

Spiral blades saw in all directions with 360° cutting capability. Excellent for 0° radius scroll/fret work — no need to turn the workpiece. Bevel cut letters and numbers.

The Olson Saw Co.
Bethel, CT 06801 USA
www.olsonsaw.com

© Copyright 2007 Olson Saw Co.

Form-OL-1052 n 4/09

Scroll Saw Blade Selection Chart

OLSON®
www.olsonsaw.com

Material   **Finish**

Material/Finish columns (left to right): Hard Wood 1/2"–3/4", Hard Wood to 1/2", Soft Wood to 1/2"–3/4", Soft Wood to 1/2", Veneer/Thin Wood to 3/16", Plywood, MDF, Particle Board, Corian 1/8"–1/2", Plastic 1/2"–3/4", Non Ferrous Metal, Aluminum, Smooth, Splinter-Free, Medium

Legend: ▨ Recommended   ▦ Can Use   ☐ Not Recommended

Olson UPC No.	Univ. No.	Width	Thickness	TPI/ No. Rev.	Tooth Style	Pilot Hole	Application
Thick Wood							
40800	–	.080"	.018"	7	Hook	3/32"	Thick wood – up to 2" without burning!
Skip Tooth							
40000	3/0	.022"	.008"	33	Skip	1/32"	Ultra intricate sawing, veining, line art, close knit jig saw puzzles
44000	2/0	.022"	.010"	28	Skip	1/32"	Extremely intricate sawing, veining, line art
44300	2	.029"	.012"	20	Skip	3/64"	Tight radius work, fretwork
44500	4	.035"	.015"	15	Skip	1/16"	Tight radius work, fretwork
44600	5	.038"	.016"	12.5	Skip	1/16"	Close radius cutting
44800	7	.045"	.017"	11.5	Skip	1/16"	General Purpose
45000	9	.053"	.018"	11.5	Skip	1/16"	General Purpose
45300	12	.062"	.024"	9.5	Skip	5/64"	Heavy duty for fast cuts
Pin End							
42401	–	.070"	.010"	18.5	Skip	3/16"	Skip style teeth/ Very thin cuts
40501	–	.100"	.018"	20	Reg.	3/16"	Regular style teeth/ thin cuts
41001	–	.100"	.018"	7	Hook	3/16"	Thick wood, up to 2" without burning!
41101	–	.100"	.018"	15	Reg.	3/16"	General purpose, regular style teeth
41201	–	.100"	.018"	10	Reg.	3/16"	Regular style teeth, fast cutting
42003	–	.100"	.018"	9/5	Skip	3/16"	Heavy duty widely-spaced set teeth for fast cutting
42701	–	.070"	.010"	25	Reg.	3/16"	Regular style teeth/ fine cuts
Double Tooth							
43200	3/0	.023"	.008"	33	Double	1/32"	Ultra intricate sawing, veining, line art, close knit jig saw puzzles
43300	2/0	.023"	.011"	37	Double	1/32"	Veining, line art & marquetry
43400	1	.026"	.013"	30	Double	3/64"	Delicate fretwork
43500	3	.032"	.014"	23	Double	3/64"	Extremely intricate sawing
43600	5	.038"	.016"	16	Double	1/16"	Tight radius work
43700	7	.044"	.018"	13	Double	1/16"	Close radius cutting
43800	9	.053"	.018"	11	Double	1/16"	General purpose
43900	12	.061"	.022"	10	Double	5/64"	Heavy duty, fast cuts
NEW! Scroll Saw Files							
42101	–	.156"	.056"	(Pin End)		3/16"	For wood, plaster, greenware, soapstone and non-ferrous metals. Turns your scroll saw into a power sander!
42100	–	.156"	.056"	(Plain End)		3/16"	

Hint! (All Blades) For best performance, use lower numbers for thinner stock and higher numbers for thicker stock.

Skip tooth blades are excellent for fast cuts that provide smooth finishes and good chip clearance. Univ No. 3/0 – 5 blade sizes can be used to cut cold rolled steel, copper, brass, aluminum sheet and bronze. Soft metal up to 1/8" thick can be cut easily, whether single sheets or several thin sheets in a stack cut.

Pin End scroll saw blades are for machines that require 5" pin end blades. They are perfect for Sears Craftsman, Penn State, Delta, Ryobi and all 15" and 16" imported scroll saws that require pin end blades.

Hint! Slow feed rate down! Relax! Let the blade do the cutting to minimize burning. Also, use a lube stick on the blade or clear shipping tape on the workpiece to inhibit scorching.

Double tooth blades have two teeth together followed by a flat space for efficient chip removal. They cut fast, leaving clean edges in wood and plastic.

Hint! (All Blades) For best performance, use lower numbers for tighter radii and higher numbers for more general purpose cuts.

The Olson Saw Co. Bethel, CT 06801 USA www.olsonsaw.com

© Copyright 2007 Olson Saw Co.

Form-OL-1052 n 4/09

Wood Burning

If you are experiencing burning while you are cutting, you are using the wrong blade. A scroll saw is unlike any other saw. It cuts in the down stroke and is supposed to clear all wood when the stroke goes up. This is why the most common blades are called skip tooth blades. The skip area allows the sawdust to escape during cut. If the teeth are too close together, the saw dust will fill the area between each tooth and will ride or burn the wood. When this happens don't just go to the next size up. Skip one or two sizes to give you a larger space between the teeth. Pushing or forcing the wood into the blade too fast can also burn the wood at times. Let the blade do the cutting without much pressure.

Remember, blades do wear out. If you have to push too hard, maybe the blade is worn out, or it could just be the wrong size.

Most Common Uses for Specific Wood

Instead of noting the generic numbers of the blades and what they could possibly cut, I have instead made a list of wood or material, plus the thickness. Then I have indicated which blade is best suited for cutting which material.

Remember these rules for proper blade selection and proper finish.

I. If you are using the right blade the left side is shiny smooth with no tear on the top or bottom of your work piece.

2. The softer the woods, the smaller the blade; the harder the wood, the larger the blade.

3. The same size milled blade or Precision Ground Tooth can be used. You will find out that the milled blades will not cut as fast.

4. The Precision Ground Tooth blade will actually cut faster and last 7 to 10 times longer than milled.

5. With the milled blades cutting slower, the resulting cut will usually end with a smoother finish on softwoods like pine.

6. For a smoother finish while cutting, go to a smaller blade. The more teeth per inch, the smoother the finished cut will be.

7. If you are trying to cut fast, going to a larger blade will not assure speed. Having the smaller blade with more teeth will sometimes cut faster with the right finish.

8. If you are getting burning, go to a larger blade. You can also slow down the feed rate of the wood. If that does not work, you can put clear packing tape on the bottom of the wood and this will help stop burning.

9. Stacking woods to increase production slows down the cut speed and you might need to increase the size of the blade for proper finish. Stacking might slow down the cut so much that it is faster to cut each piece of wood individually.

10. Crown Tooth blades are the very best for cutting plastic.

11. If you cut thick plastic and it melts, spray a lubricant such as WD-40 on your pattern and you will have a smooth finish.

12. I have saved the **most important tip** for last. It is, let the blade do the cutting. Do not push too fast or the finish will suffer.

Material	Thickness	Blade Size
Veneer	All	2/0
Pine	Up to ¼"	2
Pine	¼" to 2"	5
Oak	Up to ¼"	5
Oak	¼" to ½"	7
Oak	½" to 2"	9
Walnut	¼" to ½"	5
Walnut	½" to ¼"	7
Walnut	¼" to 2"	9
Birch	Up to ¼"	7
Birch	¼" to 2"	9
Cherry	Up to ¼"	7
Cherry	¼" to 2"	9
Popular	Up to ¼"	5
Popular	¼" to 2"	7
Maple	Up to ¼"	5
Maple	¼" to ½"	7
Maple	½" to 2"	9
Cedar	Up to ½"	5
Cedar	½" to 2"	7
Mahogany	Up to ½"	7
Mahogany	½" to 2"	9
Exotics	Up to ½"	7
Exotics	½" to 2"	9
¼" Plywood		5
½" Plywood		7
3/4" Plywood		9
Masonite	Up to ¼"	5
Masonite	¼" to ½"	7
Plastic	Up to ⅛"	5 Crown
Plastic	⅛" to ¼"	7 Crown
Plastic	¼" to ½"	9 Crown
Plastic	½" to I"	12 Crown
Corian	¼"	7
Corian	½" to ¾"	9

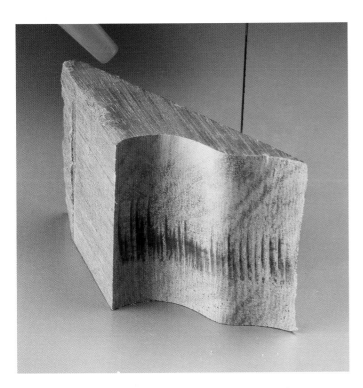

Example of wood burning during the cutting process

Trouble Shooting

Problem	Solution
Blade breaking in the middle	Tighten the next blade
Noisy saw	Tighten blade tension. Check all bolts in the stand
Side of cut not smooth enough	Use a smaller sized blade, or slow down the feed rate
Saw cuts on an angle	See if blade is at 90 degree to table; see if table is warped. Use a false table.
Wood will not come out either side	Tighten blade tension.

Achieving Mastery

Technique in Cutting

The question most often asked is, "How do you cut like that?" I have found a simple technique over the years for teaching a person to cut successfully that is really easy to learn, with only a little practice time required.

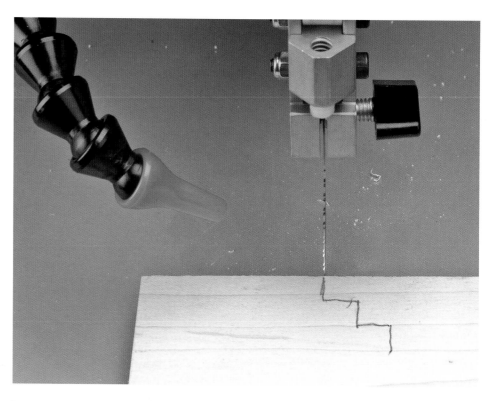

1 First, draw a stair step with six 90° turns on any scrap wood you have. Second, slow your saw down. You will find that it is much easier to turn and learn at a lower speed.

2 Now here is the real secret: You *do not* want to hold the wood with both hands like you would a steering wheel. Point at something with your left hand. Then put your hand down while pointing and place it on the wood next to the line you want to cut. The pointing finger should be about one inch away from the side of the blade while cutting. *Do not let any other finger on that hand touch the wood, ESPECIALLY YOUR THUMB.* This finger will do one of three things while holding the wood down. It will either: 1) Push the wood forward to cut or 2) Hold the wood still or 3) Pull the wood while the saw is running. Then it will push

left or right depending on which way the line goes. Now with your right hand you can take hold of the wood any way you want to. The key is only turning the wood with one hand (your right) while the other (left pointing finger) directs whether or not the blade cuts. It is hard for people to realize you do not have to be pushing into the blade at all times. You can hold the wood in one spot and the blade will just sit there.

3 If you are left-handed then use your right finger for the hold down and grab the wood with your left.

Think of it this way: When you first learn how to drive you hold the wheel with two hands. You can always tell a new driver while following from behind. They are always compensating, turning the wheel to the left or right. Now, having much greater experience, when you drive you have much better control with using only one hand for turning. Now cut down into the wood by pushing the wood forward with the left hand and the right hand controlling the wood to stay on the line. Stop pushing in when you get to the bottom of the first step. With the

left hand and one finger down, push in the direction the line goes. That is to the right. You will notice that the blade is not cutting but riding on the left side that does not cut.

With a standard blade you know that it only cuts in the front. There are not any teeth on the left side, the back and the right side.

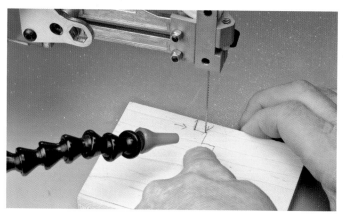

4 Now, while the saw is still running, you want to turn to the right. Push in the direction the line goes with your left finger and turn the wood with your right hand, and keep the pressure against the blade until it lines up with the line you want to cut. You will notice that the pressure goes from the left side of the blade to the back of the blade and does not cut. It just rides in that space until you push it back into the teeth. If you did this right you have a 90° right turn.

5 Now cut until the next turn.

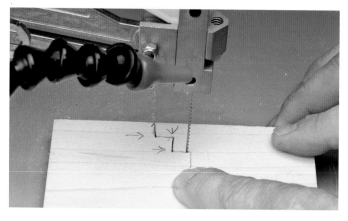

6 You will have to turn left. Again, with your left finger put pressure in the direction the line goes. This time you will actually have to pull the wood toward the right side of the blade. Keep the pressure against the blade again until the line is in front of the teeth.

7 Then push the wood into the teeth to cut forward. Another 90° turn should show. If you can do both cuts easily you are really lucky. I have found that most people can turn one way really easily but have a hard time turning the other.

8 In fact most people do turns to the right easily but have a hard time turning to the left. Most of the left turns look more like an elbow, rather than a 90° turn. Do not let this bother you. In hands on classes, every person has elbows in turns going one way or the other. Just remember this: *Keep the pressure in the direction the line goes the whole time you are turning the wood. Do not let the wood go into the teeth to cut while turning.* This will insure that your turns are 90° and have no elbows.

If you use this technique, you will see how your corners are smoothed and polished by the sides of the blade.

If you cut and the wood jumps and chatters on the table, it is usually because you are letting the blade go forward while in a tight turn. Put more pressure on the sides that do not cut and the teeth will not grab during the turn.

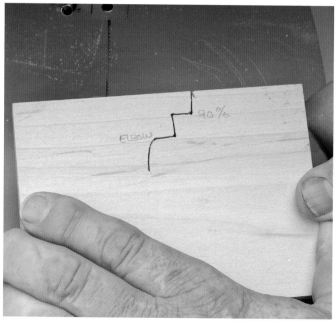

Patterns

There is an endless search for patterns. I have found patterns to cut in pictures in just about any magazine I have read. There is a great selection of pattern books available on the market today. Some children's patterns come out of coloring books. I have found the best sources of patterns, patterns that have not been seen by other woodworkers, are iron on transfer pattern books. You can get these from fabric stores. They look like telephone books with 10,000 different patterns and are ordered by subject. If you like the pattern, you can make it larger or smaller at the copier.

When you have decided on a pattern, make a copy. I do not like to trace patterns with tracing paper because I lose part of each pattern if I miss the line. Then, when I cut with my saw, I again lose part of the pattern as I missed that line. So, in my experience, you take double the chance of not duplicating the pattern if you take that extra step and copy the pattern onto tracing paper. So, my advice is you just make a photocopy instead. Glue this copy to your material instead. I use a glue stick to attach the pattern to the wood. People use all different kinds of glue. There is a good reason why I use a glue stick. This glue is water-

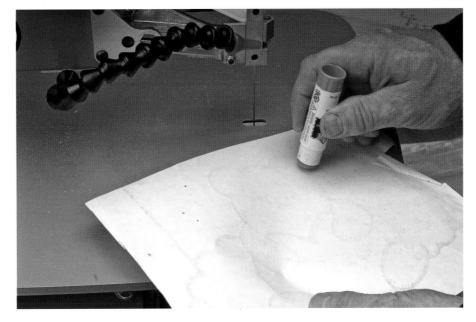

soluble. This means if you do not get all the glue off small pieces, and you want to paint them, the base coat that goes on first usually dilutes the glue. The other reason I use a glue stick is that I can really direct the glue to the point where I want it to stick. I have tried using spray adhesive, but it goes everywhere, even places I don't need it to stick. This just increases sanding and it repels paint if left on the wood.

The only time I use any other glue is if I don't want the picture to come off the material. Then I will use white glue or spray adhesive. If you cut within a few minutes of applying glue stick adhesive to the paper, the paper will peel right off. After an hour or so, when I cut, if the paper doesn't come off, then a little water from a rag will make the glue let go and the paper comes right off.

Making Templates

Templates are used only if I have to cut a large number of copies from a single pattern. I have used templates made of cardboard, plastic, metal, and wood up to 3/4" thick. I have found 1/8" Masonite to work the best. I will put the photocopy on the Masonite and put the saw on a very slow speed. This ensures easy cutting while trying to stay on the line. Remember, when you want to be exact, slow your saw down. It is much easier to steer when the saw is set to a slow speed.

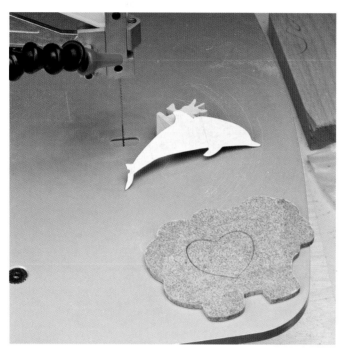

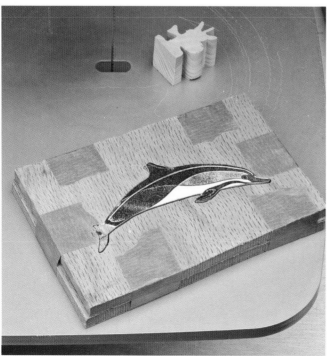

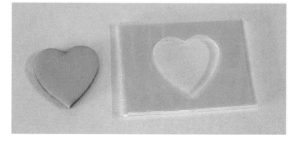

Sometimes I have wanted to reproduce a lot of an item with very small inside cuts and cannot get a pencil into the template cut to trace it. When this happens, I cut the template out of aluminum. I use the aluminum from the hardware store that is used for flashing. It is the perfect thickness, it is sturdy, and yet you can trace in small turns easily. When you cut it, place the aluminum between two 1/16th or 1/8th inch Masonite pieces and cut your pattern from that. This holds the aluminum and you will not have any bending on the edges.

When I make small templates, I make them in two different fashions. I use one template just to cut out the pattern outline and then trace around it. The other template includes the pattern in the middle of the material and allows me to trace the inside of the template. This is just easier than trying to trace around my fingers while holding the template.

Cutting Different Material

Softwood or pine is probably the most common material cut with a scroll saw. The most common blade for pine is a *#5* as it cuts the quickest and provides the best finish. If you use a #7, it will cut fast but you sacrifice the finish. If I want to have a glass finish, I will use a #2, but the speed of the cut is greatly diminished.

When cutting hardwoods, a #9 blade is the most common. A #7 blade might burn instead of providing a smooth cut. When you cut hardwood, you automatically get a smooth cut or a burn. There is not much choice in blades. It mostly depends on the thickness of the hardwood you are cutting when trying to use a smaller blade. If you use thin wood, you can use a thinner blade. Some people say they use a certain blade for cutting hardwood but that they put packing tape on the back to stop the burning. I will try to tell you what blade to use to avoid burning without having to use another trick to get the finish you want.

To increase production, I will stack wood. When using thin wood, I hold the wood together with masking tape spaced about two inches apart around the wood. I tape it this way because it holds all the wood together without creating any void between the wood. If you use double face tape or carpet tape in between the layers of wood, you will get tearing on all of the pieces of wood because of that space the tape creates. I have also found that once I stack the material higher than 1 inch, the speed of cuts drop greatly. In trying to cut two 3/4" patterns at once, I discovered the cutting process actually took longer than it did cutting each piece of wood separately. You would have to use a larger blade to stop burning problems, and then you would not get the smooth cut that stems from the ease of turning that a small blade provides.

Cutting Plastic

Successfully cutting plastic and not having it melt back together while you cut depends on what saw you use. As stated earlier, the stroke of your saw does make a difference. If you have a saw with a short stroke, it will melt plastic faster than a saw with a long stroke. To cut plastic successfully, you will have to use some of the tricks that you are about to learn.

Plastic usually comes with paper on both sides to keep down scratching. Cutting the plastic with this paper remaining in place is a must to stop plastic meltdown. Some plastic comes with paper on one side and a thin, clear plastic on the other, so you can see the color. If this is how your plastic is packaged, cut the plastic with the paper side down. The problem with this is you cannot draw a pattern on the covering plastic and sometimes glue stick does not hold and a pattern will not stay in place. To remedy this situation, you need to cover the clear plastic side with masking tape. With the masking tape in place, you can draw on the thin layer of clear plastic or glue will stick to the masking tape, and this layer of tape will also help to stop meltdown.

So this is trick number 1. If your saw has a short stroke, apply masking tape on each side of the plastic you chose to cut. Apply this tape on top of the existing paper covering the plastic. As the blade goes through the masking tape, it keeps the hot plastic from coming back and melting back together. If you cut thick plastic or stack thin plastic together, you might have meltdown even with masking tape on both sides. 2. Spray a lubricant on top of your pattern. I use W-D 40. It does not have oils in it. W-D 40 goes down through the plastic with each stroke and helps the plastic to come out smoother. If your cut takes a long time, the W-D 40 might evaporate. If this happens, just spray on a little more W-D 40 and keep cutting.

As a cautionary note: Once while cutting the W-D 40 did evaporate and I just reached over and grabbed some oil. When the blade hit that oil, the plastic it fused to the blade. I ended up breaking the plastic and the blade while trying to get them apart. So remember, use a lubricant and *not oil* on plastic.

Use the new Crown Tooth blades and you will really stop the plastic from melting. I can't stress enough how well the Crown Tooth blade cuts plastic. You get a nice clean and clear finish.

Metal Cutting

There are special blades for metal cutting. They can be identified easily because there is not any space between the teeth. (See the blade list.) Like the wood cutting blades, you want them tight in tension so you will get a straight cut. In metal cutting you especially do not want the blade to wander.

You need a saw that will slow down when cutting metal. If you run the blade speed too fast, it will heat the blade up prematurely and it will soon break. With the blade speed too slow, you will have a tough time holding the metal down while the blade is on the up stroke. Depending on the hardness and the thickness of the metal, you will have to speed it up or slow it down. The secret is to set a speed where you can follow the line and still not wear the blade out.

You can cut any non-ferrous material up to 3/8 of an inch thick. When cutting copper or brass, if it is thick enough, you will not have to support the underside with another material like 1/8 Masonite. If it is thin, then you have to sandwich it between two pieces of Masonite or any other thin material. This Masonite keeps the metal from bouncing up and down during the cutting. If the material is thin, then use a #5 PGT blade to cut through the wood and metal. The PGT blade is harder then any other blade out there and it cuts the wood and metal with a nice clean cut.

When cutting aluminum, no matter what the thickness, it will usually bend down or warp on both sides of the cut. To prevent this, I sandwich the aluminum between some thin materials. This material can be as thin as 1/8 Masonite on both sides. With the aluminum sandwiched, this gives you something that your pattern will stick to and it also makes handling the aluminum easier. I will use a PGT blade most of the time when cutting aluminum, no matter what the thickness. When cutting small pieces of metal, like coins, I use packing tape to hold those small pieces of metal down to another piece of wood.

3

Projects

Puzzles

Puzzles can be made in many different ways:

1. Stand up style.
2. Locking puzzles that stand.
3. Flat locking.
4. Flat individual pieces.

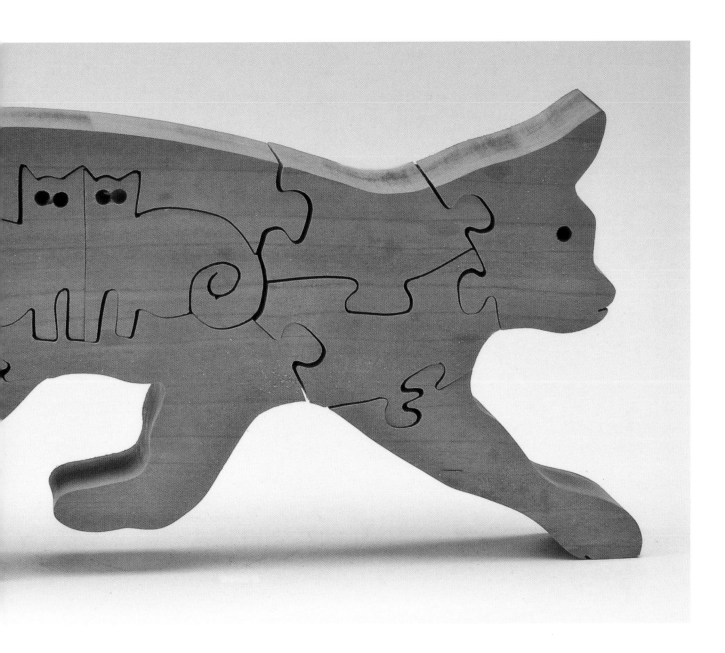

Stand up style puzzles are usually among the first projects beginning scroll saw artists create. You can cut an animal pattern out and stand it up. Then cut the animal into individual puzzles pieces. There is just one thing to remember when cutting puzzles. If you want them to stay together, you have to make sure each piece has at least two curves on each piece of the puzzle. I call them "mushrooms." There are two types of mushrooms that can be used on each piece. Mushrooms can be cut in or cut out on any given piece. You have to have at least two mushrooms per piece or the puzzle will not hold itself together.

When cutting puzzles, keep this in mind for blade usage. Use the smallest blade possible to insure a good, snug fit. When cutting puzzles for children, use larger blades so the pieces will slide apart and back together easily.

Locking puzzles that stand are puzzle that will not come apart unless you take out a wooden locking pin. Patterns such as a snake or a fish work well for standing, locking puzzles. The longer the pattern is, the better it works as a locking puzzle. Put a number on opposite sides to indicate sides 1 and 2. Starting with side number one, and cut the mushroom in the center of the wood. Take this piece off. Turn the wood from side A ¼ turn to side B and cut the next mushroom, again in the center, so it cuts into the first mushroom cut but only half way through it. Take this piece off and turn it back to side 1. Cut another mushroom into the last mushroom. Make sure the mushrooms are always in the middle of the wood so they will be in the finished project. Continue this process until the puzzle is long enough for your pattern. Now cut out the pattern you want. This puzzle will have to be put back in order of the last cut. Then drill a hole for the eye through the first mushroom and put in a dowel to lock it all together.

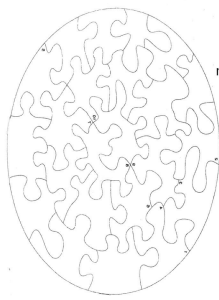

Flat puzzles have to be the most common puzzles and, for me, the most profitable. You can take a picture of anything and glue it to a piece of wood and cut it into a puzzle. I use a spray adhesive for gluing the picture down. Again, use the two mushrooms rule for each piece you cut. They can be, and will usually be, all different sizes. Take pictures of family reunions or just individual pictures and glue them to some nice Birch plywood. Using thinner wood is usually better. If you want to make a puzzle unique, cut small shapes into the puzzle while making it. I will cut pictures within the picture, including houses, whales, boots, palm trees, and even witches on brooms. This adds value, as well as entertainment, to the puzzles.

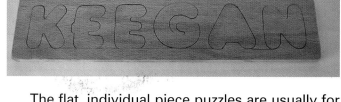

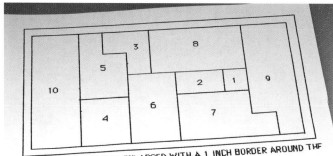

THIS PUZZLE SHOULD BE ENLARGED WITH A 1 INCH BORDER AROUND THE EDGE.

The flat, individual piece puzzles are usually for making names or educational puzzles for children. These puzzles are often of the numbers 1 through 10 and the alphabet. I even cut one that was made up of the 12 shapes children learn on television. I make these puzzles out of ¼" Birch plywood and paint them a solid color with a water based paint and spray them with a gloss finish. I have found that if you use thicker then ½" wood, the children have a hard time lining up the shape to fall into the hole. The thinner the wood, the easier it falls into place. So use ¼" wood if possible.

Three Dimensional Projects

Deer

There are different ways to make three-dimensional projects. The most popular and widely used is probably the deer. You can really cut anything, as long as you can visualize both sides of its profile.

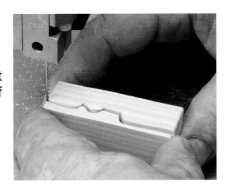

1 First cut out one side profile of the deer.

2 Next cut the other side profile, making it as close to a mirror image of the profile on the first side as you can.

3 Then cut the inside of the antlers.

4 Cut in between the legs.

5 Remove the excess wood from one side of the deer and lay it down on the flat surface of the excess wood on the other side. This gives you a flat surface to cut the front profile of the deer.

6 Then cut out in between the legs, ...

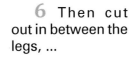

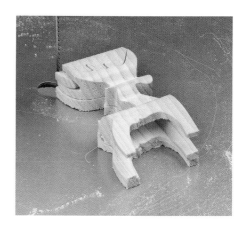

7... and now the back and the antlers.

You now have your first deer!

You can draw it on the wood if you want, but try it without the pattern once and you will see how easy it really is, even without a pattern.

Duck

Let's cut a duck.

First you cut the front view of the duck like the deer. But this time, when you are done, the two outside pieces are not apart. You will have to cut them apart so you can see the profile; just cut when you put it on the side.

Now you can cut the side profile.

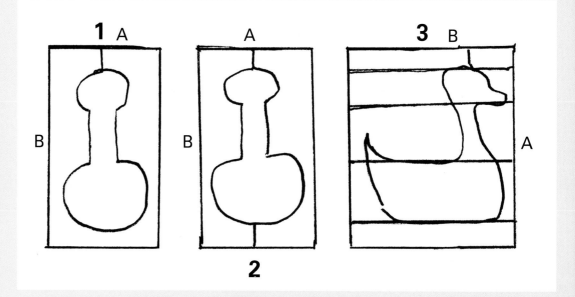

Another way of making a three-dimensional cut is by using the veining method that the Scrollers of Chicago made famous. You take a picture and cut out the pattern with lines created by your blade and this helps make the picture.

Now cut other pieces of the same picture so you can set them on top of small pieces of wood or on the first cut you make (per example).

Putting the picture together in layers gives you part of the three-dimensional look.

The veining gives you another depth. You will use a #2/0 blade in cutting the lines or veins to show the picture. Veining is cutting from the outside of the wood, following lines to accent the picture, but stopping before you cut through to keep the piece in one whole piece. The little girl holding the pot is an example. In doing this veining, you usually have no inside cuts. This is great because you can really cut a lot of pictures by stacking them 2 or 3 deep. And you never have to take the blade out for inside cuts. If you are cutting a new picture you have designed yourself, make sure you do not cut the veins too close to each other or you will make the picture structurally weak. If you want to cut a line that goes across the whole picture, just cut in 40 degree in each direction with 20 degree left in the center for stability.

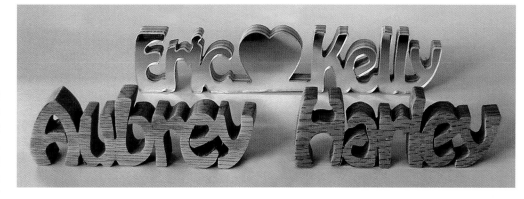

Cutting Names

Cutting names is the most profitable project in scrolling. Everyone likes to see his or her name. It helps children learn in puzzles and identifies an executive at his or her desk. You can personalize a clock by putting in the name of a family. Use the first names of a newly wed couple, with an accompanying picture, for a trivet. Whenever you use some ones name, it becomes special for that person.

You can start with names for the top of a desk. Just the name cut will go anywhere. You can do this several ways, but the most common is with a template. You can get these from a company called Sayeo Sales out of Texas. They are cut out of a plastic. There are three different sizes of plastic templates. They come in one inch, one and a half-inch, and two inch sizes. The one and a half-inch templates are the most popular. The one-inch is usually used inside patterns. I only use the two-inch when I want to cut a name for outdoors. It is big enough to be seen far away.

Plastic templates never wear out and are made so each letter touches each other for easy cutting. There is one thing I do to make the cutting of names fast and easy. A lot of people put the letter of the template at the bottom of the wood and cut after that. You have to cut into and out of the bottom of each letter. This creates a lot of potential for sanding later. Instead, draw a line on the wood ¼" from the bottom and draw the letters on the line. Cut into the wood starting between two letters and then cut the rest of the name without having to stop. I will even cut into the center of the letter "O" or the top of a (E) or (P) and then keep on cutting. It does not take away from the name at all. Then when you are done the name is smooth and flat with no sanding required.

Now take the wood you just cut with a name and place it onto a small piece of wood routed around the edges. This usually looks good with off colors of wood. Pick a light colored wood for the name and a dark colored wood for the stand.

I have seen a person type names on the computer and then transfer this to the wood. You can pick any font and size you want. Then just glue it down with a glue stick and cut it out.

If you want to cut a name with a different twist, cut the bottom of the wood where you have drawn the name at a 30 degree angle. Then cut the name out and place it on a base. This tilts the name up to the people who are looking down at it, and it is perfect for a desk name.

If you want to use a spiral blade, you can make a very unusual nameplate. After drawing out the name, tilt the table 20° to the right. Cutting with a spiral blade, cut the whole name out without spinning the wood. This will cut the name at one

angle. You can only get this using a spiral blade. Again make sure the blade is tensioned twice. Once when you start and again after you cut 2" to get the tension back.

Key chain names can be very popular. First pre-cut your wood to be one inch tall. Oak is the wood that is most popular. Each letter is one inch tall and usually one-half inch wide. The letters "m" or "w" measure one inch by one inch. They are just block capital letters. They are cut from the bottom and the top to achieve different sizes. Take pictures of family reunions or just individual pictures and glue them to some nice Birch plywood. Using thinner wood is usually better.

You will not have any inside cuts. The holes in the letters like the "e" or and "a" are usually done with a drill. You do have some sanding because of the in and out cutting on the bottom and top. There is just one thing to note, when putting in the eye screw that holds the ring, make sure you drill a small hole. Make sure it is large enough so the wood does not split, but small enough so the screw will hold tight.

Fretwork

Fretwork is the most time consuming cutting that you can do with your saw. It takes time because of the stopping and starting involved in changing the blade. If you have a saw that makes is hard to get the blade through the hole, it will take even longer to complete the cutting. This is where you will want the quick release for the top of your saw. You will spend twice as much time moving the blade into and out of the holes as you will spend in cutting, and the cutting will take hours.

Some fretwork has such small cuts you will wonder where you may drill the hole for the blade to fit through. If at all possible, drill the hole away from the side of the cut so it does not tear or fray the wood with the bit. Always use the largest drill bit possible. The easier it is to get the blade through the wood, the quicker the project gets done. When cutting from the hole to the final line, approach it at 90 degrees. You approach the line at 90 degrees so, when you come back to the starting spot on the line, it is easier to match up the cut line without the blade jumping off line. I always cut on the line when possible. Then when you have finished that cut and come back to the starting place, it is easier to match the two cuts up flush.

When working on projects like clocks and other fretwork you will be cutting two pieces of wood at a time for a lot of the projects. There are different ways to hold the wood together. I will cut two pieces of

wood in the shape desired and hold these together with masking tape. I attach tape every two inches, holding the wood firmly together. I do not use double sided tape placed between the two pieces of wood. This approach leaves a space or void between the two pieces of wood and causes the wood to fray or splinter in between each piece. If you use double-sided tape, you also have to get the wood apart after cutting. The double tape does such a good job sticking together that I have seen people break the fret work apart after hours of cutting. Using nails destroys part of the wood you are trying to cut. They even come through the bottom of the wood and will catch on or scratch your table. Masking tape goes on easy and comes off easy.

Pictures on Plastic

Items needed for this project are: 1/8" to ¼" white plastic, spray adhesive, a picture or photo, and a number 2 blade.

Putting pictures on plastic can really be used for many different projects. You can use them as refrigerator magnets. They can sit or stand-alone or you can glue them to other plastic for cardholders. The key is the picture, which personalizes whatever you cut for that person.

I have tried all colors of plastic and found white to be the best for cutting pictures. The white color does not take away from the colors of the picture. Clear plastic does not quite set off the color of the picture like white does.

Along with the white plastic and the picture you want to cut, you will need some brand of spray

adhesive. I have found all of the different brands to work just fine.

Plastic usually comes with paper on both sides. Take the paper off of one side of the plastic. Spray the glue on that side of the plastic and onto the back of the picture. Let them sit for 2 to 3 minutes, then glue the plastic and the image together. Make sure you remove all of the air pockets. I usually use a rubber roller for that part.

Put your saw on a very slow speed for accurate cutting. Use a regular #2 skip tooth blade for this project. Do not use a reverse tooth blade as it frays the picture. If your saw will not slow down and the plastic melts, you can spray a lubricant on the picture like WD-40. This will not hurt the image, but will stop the melting. *(Sample may be seen in the gallery section, p46)*

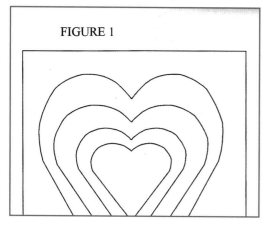

Shadow Box Effect

The first project in the classes I teach, after teaching basic cutting techniques, is a shadow box. Take a piece of wood 3 inches high by 4 inches wide. In the middle and on the bottom trace out a heart about one and a half inched tall. You can use any wood you want, but I have found that a hardwood works best in this project. I use oak or mahogany, but not pine or popular.

Tilt your table to the left 3 degrees. With the table tilted to the left, you will cut in a clockwise direction. After you have cut out the heart, you will notice it comes out in just one direction, through the top. If you let it fall down, it locks, sticking out about ¼ of an inch. Take the heart out and cut another without drawing it just ¼" outside the first one. Repeat this until you have cut five hearts out.

FIGURE 1

FIGURE 2

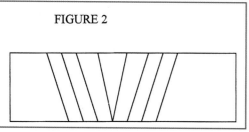

Put all the pieces in and let them fall back and lock in. Notice how the project draws your attention to the middle or the first heart you cut. This is the shadow box effect. You can do this with a picture of anything you want. I will take a picture of someone standing in the middle of any background. First, cut up around the person in the middle. Then, repeat this process five times. Again, you will see the finished project draws your attention to the person. I have even cut pictures for car shows or wedding.

Scroll Saw Box

Items needed for this project are: 2 x 2 square wood 4 inches long; a drill with a small drill bit; a number 9 blade, which will give you the clearance needed for the lid to slide and the key to come out. Make sure the table is set at 90 degrees to the table. If not, the key and lid will not slide out as easily as it should, or not at all. Keep adequate tension on the blade to prevent belly cuts, or the lid will not slide out on either side.

Most woodworkers have seen some form of "band saw" box. Using a similar technique, you can easily make a "scroll saw" box. The best part about a scroll saw box is the locking lid. With a band saw you must cut into the box and glue it back together.

Get a nice piece of 2 x 4 about 4 inches in length. Cut this in half to form two pieces approximately 2"x 2" x 4" long. You need only one of these pieces. Save the other piece to make another box later on. You have both pieces with two round corners and two straight corners where you cut them in half.

On the side of the two straight corners, draw a straight line ¼" across the top and the bottom the length of the 4 inches. This will end up being the top and bottom cuts.

Cut the bottom first. Set it aside. Now flip over the block 1/4 turn so that side A (the side) is towards you and side B (top side) is on top. Cut a pattern of your choice into side A near the end of the block. This forms the key. The illustration in the Exhibit shows a tulip. You may prefer to cut a letter to make the box a little more personal.

After cutting the key, remove it and set it aside with the bottom piece. Flip the block back over ¼ turn so the side A is up once again. You will see the parallel opening or slot formed by cutting out the key. Now, you are ready to cut the top off. As you cut down the line drawn, you can feel a difference in feed pressure as you pass by the slot the key left. Once you're a little past the key slot, cut a puzzle pattern into the body. For more lid stability, cut two puzzle patterns. Slide the lid or top off and put it with the key and bottom slice.

With the lid and bottom pieces removed, drill a hole through the middle of the top surface where the lid is to be attached. Cut out the box interior area. Make sure you do not cut out the key area or the key will slip into the box, preventing lock up.

After cutting out the box area, glue the bottom slice back on. If done carefully, you will not even see where the blade cut the bottom off! Give it time to dry.

Slide the top on and insert the key. Sand the sides and corners so they are rounded like the others and you have a "scroll saw" box.

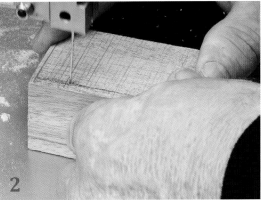

5

6

7

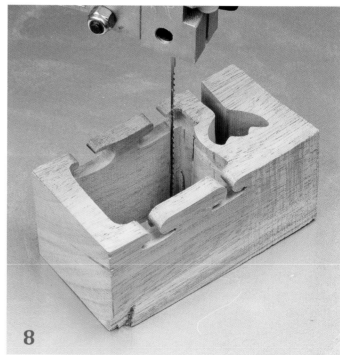

8

9

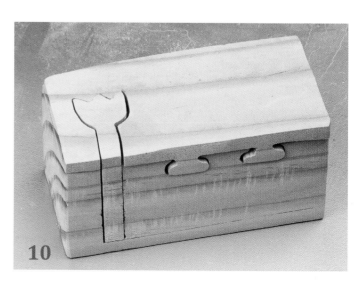

10

40

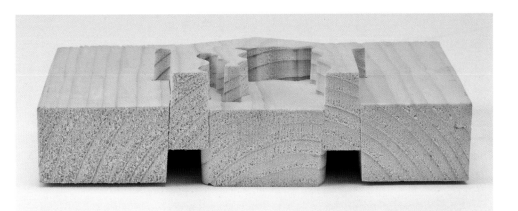

Bevel Cutting

To understand how the saw cuts while the table is tilted, first try this cut. Take a piece of wood, with your table tilted at 25 degrees to the left, cut into it one inch and then turn 90 degrees to the right in cutting. I call this turning the wood up hill. Now cut only 1/8 of and inch and then try to turn while cutting back 180 degrees. With the table tilted to the left you cannot turn to the left sharply while cutting. I call this turning the wood down hill. Look at the piece of wood you just cut. If you cut all the way around, the wood will be shaped like a cone. The wood is a large circle on the top and comes to a point on the bottom. Remember this while cutting and the table is tilted even 2 or 3 degrees, "It is easy turning the wood up hill on the table to get a 90 degree angle, but impossible when turning the wood down hill on the table." With the table just tilted 2 degrees, it is real close to being 90 degree turns each way, but the more you tilt the table, the bigger the circle when turning up hill on the table. Tilting your table like you did in the shadow box can give you a three-dimensional look to your cutting. To understand this, first make a simple cut. Tilt your table to the left 3 degrees. Cutting in a clockwise direction cut out a cat. Now in the opposite direction cut a house around the cat. The cat will lock in, falling back, and the house will lock in falling forward. It looks like the cat is inside the house, even though only the house is out towards you and the cat is actually even with the other wood not cut.

Cut out a scene using a piece of wood 3 inches tall and 4 inches long. Start the scene cut from the left. Cut the lawn, the house, more lawn, a tree, some flowers and then cut out. Now in the opposite direction cut a cloud, a lightening bolt, some more clouds and finish the cut. Again you will see that the center of the three pieces falls away from the outside two pieces of wood and gives you a three dimensional look

Veneer-Marquetry

When you first learn how to use your saw, you can cut veneer. There are just a few requirements and you can make beautiful Marquetry pictures to enhance any furniture, or just create pictures with Marquetry.

Requirement number one: your saw has to have a slow speed. You cannot cut the thin veneer and follow the lines if it does not go lower then 400 strokes per minute. Requirement number two: you have to make a false table. This is usually a piece of ¼ material that covers the whole scroll saw table, including the hole that the blade goes through. Again I usually make this out of Masonite. One side is usually smooth.

Make the false table so that it hangs at least two inches over each side of the main table, that is two inches on both the left and right sides. The false table should cover the table from the very back to at least two inches longer then the front. Now, with a number *5* blade in the saw, cut the false table down the middle of the wood until the table hits the back arms of the saw. The number *5* blade is used to make a cut wide enough for the 2/0 blade to fit through when the table is tilted. This cut will make it easier placing the table on and taking it off without taking out the blade.

Now while the false table is in place, mark under the false table on both sides and in the front where the original table stops. Take the false table off and glue small pieces of wood where you marked it. These added pieces of wood will hold the table so it will not move or slide while you are cutting.

Now you need tracing paper, a pencil, a razor blade knife, marquetry tape, masking tape, and a pattern to draw onto the wood.

I could devote a whole book on Marquetry, but here we will just give the basics. Whenever you cut veneer, you use a 2/0 blade. This gives you the best cut with a smooth finish. The type of cutting I use for Marquetry is called bevel cutting. Using this method when you put the wood together, you do not see any space where the blade cut. All the wood fits next to each other as each cut is at 13 degrees, using the number 2/0 blade. Unlike creating an inlay, we know the exact blade and the thickness of the wood. We know a 13-degree tilt in the table is what makes the wood snap in flush with the other wood.

Start with one part of the picture and trace it onto the wood where you want it to be cut out. Look at the wood and see how the grain can accent your picture. Just by having the grain of the wood go in different directions, you can create a three-dimensional looks to your picture. Use the different colors of the wood to show shadows. Knots in the wood can really help when making eyes or other points that you want accented in a picture.

Next place that picture on the wood on top of the next piece of wood you want it to fit with for the next part of the picture. Tape them together so you can keep them together as one until the cutting is done. Cut through the two pieces of wood only where they will join. Using marquetry tape, tape the two pieces of wood that you want to be the picture together on the backside. Notice how they slide together and you cannot see any space between the wood. Because the wood is cut at an angle (like this /1) at the same time, the two pieces fit together. Turn the two back over and draw out the second part of the picture. Repeat this process as you add one piece of wood to the others and tape them together to form your picture.

Inlay

Inlay is when you cut two pieces of wood at the same time, on a bevel or angle, and one of the cut pieces of wood fits into the other tightly, as if they grew together. Often I use two different shades or colors of wood. In my example, I use Maple and Cedar. Here are the necessary steps to create inlay:

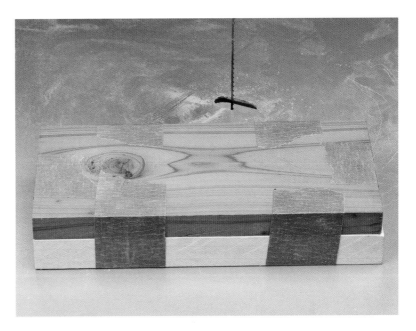

1. Tape the two woods together on all four sides so they will not move while cutting.

2. Start by tilting the table to the left around 4 degrees.

3. Make sure you inlay the thinner piece of wood into the thicker if the two pieces are not of the same thickness.

4. Cut into the wood that you want to be the finished project and make a circle and cut out. DO NOT come out in the same line you cut into the wood. Now you take out both pieces. Look at the end and you will see a wedge effect with the top being wider than the bottom. Now slip the top piece back into both and see if it will stop even with the top of the bottom piece. If it locks in just a little bit above the bottom piece this is also okay. (If so, you can go to the next step.)

If the two pieces are not even or the inset pieces is not slightly above the other piece after the top piece is inserted, go back and adjust the table. You will need to do one of two adjustments:

1. If the inset piece of wood drops past the line of the second piece, increase the angle of your cut.

2. If it stops high above the line of the second piece, decrease the angle of the cut.

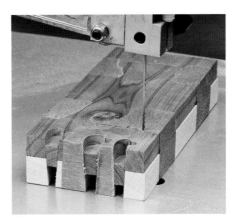

5. Drill a hole into both pieces of wood. I usually place the wood on the scroll saw table and use a hand drill. I try to drill straight down so the blade will be at the same angle as the hole I drill.

6. If you want to have the top piece of wood drop into the bottom piece, you have to cut in a clock wise direction. (Remember when you are bevel cutting and your table was tilted to the left, if you cut in the clockwise direction the wood will drop down. If you cut in the counterclockwise direction, the piece goes up.)

7. You can see in the picture that I have cut a figure out. When I put the bottom cut out into the top, you can see space all around between the figure and the outer piece.

When you put the top piece into the bottom, it wedges in. If it is a little high, push down hard. This helps wedge the piece into place and you fill the blade space with the wood. You can always sand the top piece off level with the bottom. When you do sand, put a drop of white glue into the hole. This will attract sawdust and fill the hole.

Basics

Gallery

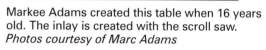

Markee Adams created this table when 16 years old. The inlay is created with the scroll saw.
Photos courtesy of Marc Adams

Photo courtesy of Marc Adams

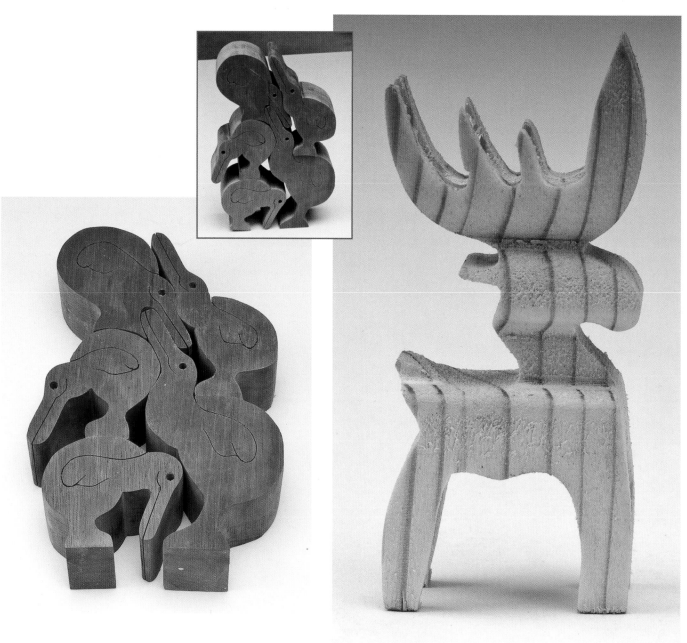

48